Preface

Efforts made in recent years to provide a wider choice of reading material for children have been warmly welcomed by teachers. Experience has shown that reading material which allows for horizontal rather than vertical movement is of paramount importance. This series aims to provide such material in the form of stories, carefully selected for their appeal to children and for their significance in the traditions and cultures of the major world religions.

Stories from World Religions, obviously not a course in religious education, can usefully supplement the material in any agreed syllabus. While it emphasises Christianity as the religion that has shaped our national life, its aim is to introduce children to the major religions as the living beliefs of other peoples of our world.

Religious truth is conveyed as much through stories as through historical events. This series therefore aims to introduce children to the different kinds of story used in religion – myth, history, legend, parable, festival – and to help children to a progressive understanding of them so that they can apprehend the truths conveyed.

The controlled vocabulary and language structure have been carefully graded to make Book 1 most suitable for reading ages 7–8 years; Book 2 for 8–9 years; Book 3 for 9–10 years; and Book 4 for 10–11 years. This has been achieved by testing each story theoretically with a recognised readability analysis, and in practice by testing with children of the appropriate reading ages.

Norman J. Bull
Reginald J. Ferris

Contents

WIDE RANGE
Stories from World Religions

3

Norman J. Bull
Reginald J. Ferris

Oliver & Boyd

Illustrated by Shirley Bellwood, Jeremy Gower,
John Harrold, Tony Herbert, Nicholas Hewetson,
Annabel Large, Michael Strand and Shirley Tourret.

Oliver & Boyd
Robert Stevenson House
1–3 Baxter's Place
Leith Walk
Edinburgh EH1 3BB

A Division of Longman Group Ltd

First published 1983

ISBN 0 05 003372 7

Set in 12/18pt Plantin 110
Printed in Hong Kong
by Sheck Wah Tong Printing Press Ltd

Stories in this Book

Everyone loves a story. When you were young you loved fairy stories, and if it was one of your favourites, you probably liked hearing it over and over again. Now you are older and you have already discovered that there are many other kinds of stories as well.

This book contains stories of different kinds, and each one tells us something about one of the great religions of the world. There are no fairy stories in this book.

History

One kind of story is about people who really lived, and about things that really happened. These real-life stories are called History. History tells us about people who really lived and about things that really happened. History is full of stories about real people. Some of them are about people who became great, and famous, and loved.

Stories of great people in history and the things they did are always popular for we want to know more about the real world, real people, and real happenings. So there are stories from history in this book.

Legends

People have always wanted to hear stories about their heroes in history, so other stories grew up about heroes and heroines. These were not real-life stories. They were Legends. Legends made a brave man seem even braver than he really was. Legends made a strong man seem even stronger than he really was. Legends made a good woman seem even better than she really was. So legends told of mighty wonders, great adventures, brave deeds, and fine actions. Although legends are told about men and women who really lived in history, and about real things in the world around us, we cannot be sure that they tell about things that really happened.

There is a legend in this book about Buddha. It tells how three animals became friends and helped each other. Buddha was a real person, but the story is a legend. The story is important, though, because it explains what Lord Buddha had said about the value of true friends.

It is important for us to know whether a story is a legend or history. That does not mean, of course, that legends have no value. Every religion has its own teaching, and legends are an important part of that teaching. They are not just good stories. They also set us examples, to show us that we can become braver or better people.

Parables

Some stories are made up specially to help us understand something else. Stories like these are called Parables. A parable puts two things side by side. It tells us about one thing, but really it is teaching us about something else. The first part of a parable is a simple story from everyday life. This helps us to understand the second part which is about

God, or about how we should live together.

One parable in this book is about a father who died and left his treasure to his three sons. They worked busily, trying to find his hoard of money, but in the end they learned that money is not the only kind of treasure.

So we must not think that parables have no value, just because they are made up. Every parable teaches us something that is important and true about God, about ourselves and about each other. So, in one sense, made-up stories like these are often far more important than stories from real life.

Myths

When we are young, the world seems very big to us and full of things we want to know about. We are curious to know more about the things around us, so we ask many questions. We want to know how things began, where they came from, and why they are here. These questions about beginnings are the hardest questions of all to answer.

People in every land have stories to answer these questions about beginnings. They are not real-life stories from history, or legends which grew up, or

8

parables which were made up. These stories tell what people long ago *believed* about how things began and why they were made. These stories of beginnings are called Myths.

One story in this book tells what Jews believed about the rainbow and how it was a sign from God. Their myth tells what the rainbow is, why it is there, and what it means.

Today we know much more about *how* things began from the discoveries of science, but science cannot tell us *why* things began. Myths tell what people long ago *believed* about the beginning of all things.

Festivals

Every year we have special times which we can share together: they are called Festivals.

Each festival has its own story, for a festival is a time of remembering and celebrating things that happened long ago—things that are so important that people never want to forget them.

During a festival, the story may be told in words, or acted in plays. It may be sung in carols, or brought to life in dance. Without the story of what happened long ago, there would be nothing to celebrate. So, of course, there would be no festivals.

In this book there is the story of the greatest festival of the year for people who follow the Hindu religion —the Festival of Diwali. There is also the story of the

greatest festival of the year for people who follow the
Christian religion—the Festival of Easter. Stories like
these show us why people want to celebrate together
at special times in the year. They explain the meaning
of festivals, and show why they are so important to
people all over the world.

Different Kinds of Stories

So there are five different kinds of stories in this
book—History, Legends, Parables, Myths and
Festival stories. All these different kinds of stories
are important and we could not do without any of
them. It is important to know the difference between
them, too, for you will be able to understand and
enjoy a story much more if you know what kind of
story it is.

Holy Places

In the Bible of the Jews, there is a story about Jacob, one of their great ancestors. On a journey through the wilderness, Jacob lay down to sleep when night came on, with only stones for a pillow. He had a dream that a ladder reached up to heaven from the place where he lay. He saw angels passing up and down the heavenly ladder, and he heard God speaking to him from above it.

When Jacob awoke, he said, "How holy is this place! It is the house of God." He made a pillar there with the stones, and he named the place Beth-el which means "House of God". And Bethel became a holy place for the people of Israel.

A place like this became holy because men and women felt God was there. People felt the presence of God in the world of nature around them, too. A mighty mountain like Mount Sinai, or Mount Fuji in Japan, must be the home of a God—a "holy place". The presence of God was felt in hills and mountains, streams and rivers, storms and tempests.

Places became holy, too, because of holy teachers. Mecca became holy to Moslems as the sacred place of their Prophet, Mohammed. Jerusalem is a holy city to Jews, Christians and Moslems. It became the custom for people to go as pilgrims to the holy places of their religion.

The religions of the world teach that God is everywhere. So people can pray to God wherever they may be. But people need special places where they can join together in worship of their God. In this book you will read about the holy places that are used for worship by people who follow the great religions of the world.

These holy places have different names. They have different shapes, too. The shape of the building often has its own meaning for the people who go there to worship God.

A place of worship is not holy because of the things used to build it, or the shape in which it is built. It is made holy by the people who set it apart for the worship of God. They often call it the "House of God", for they feel that God is present there with them—just as Jacob did at Bethel.

Mighty Marduk
slays the Monster

Every religion, whether it has one God or many, tells
of how the world began. This story comes from the
people of the ancient city of Babylon, which once
stood in the south of the country we now call Iraq.
Marduk was the city god of the people of Babylon.

*   *   *   *   *   *

In the beginning, there was nothing but water. There
were sweet waters named Apsu. They were calm and
peaceful. There were salt waters named Tiamat. They
raged and boiled. They had no order, no peace.

Now the waters of Apsu mixed with the waters of
Tiamat, and became Father and Mother of a great
host of gods. One of the chief of these gods was Ea.
He tried to keep order amongst the younger gods,
who were noisy and restless.

Before long, however, there was trouble. Father
Apsu, Father of all the gods, was growing old and
tired. He could not stand the noise of the young gods,
and he wanted peace. He complained to Mother
Tiamat. "Because of them I get no peace by day, and
no sleep by night," he said bitterly.

Tiamat could see what Apsu was thinking—he wanted to get rid of the young gods! "Why should we destroy those we have created?" she asked angrily.

Ea heard their argument, and he too could see that Apsu intended to destroy the young gods. Now Ea was clever and had magic powers. He used his magic to charm Apsu into a deep sleep. Then he slew him.

Tiamat was furious, and so were the young gods. "Apsu, our great Father, has been slain!" they cried to Mother Tiamat. "Rise up! Avenge him! Destroy his evil murderer and save us!"

Stirred to vengeance by the young gods, Tiamat prepared for war against Ea. She raised up a terrible army of fearsome monsters: poisonous serpents, fiery dragons, bloodthirsty dogs, scorpion-men, fish-men, and many others. It was so terrible an army that the young gods themselves were frightened, and joined Ea against Tiamat.

But Ea himself was too afraid of savage Tiamat to stand up to her on his own. He sent for his eldest son Marduk, a mighty warrior. He promised Marduk the divine powers of the gods if he would do battle with Tiamat.

Mighty Marduk was eager for the fray. But before he would fight, he said that the gods must make him their king. At once an assembly of the gods was called. They gave Marduk a throne, a royal robe and a sceptre, so that Marduk could rule over all the gods, and over the world of men and women. The fate of all living creatures was now in his hands.

Then Marduk went to war against Tiamat and her terrible army. The whirlwind was his chariot, drawn by four monster steeds. He was armed with his bow, and his club of thunder. Red was smeared on his face, because the gods believed that this would protect him from powers of evil. Sweet-smelling herbs protected him from the awful smell of Tiamat's horrible host. Howling winds surrounded him— tempest, hurricane and tornado. Over his arm was a great net that he had made, with a wind at each of its corners. Even the terrible monsters of Tiamat were filled with fear when they saw mighty Marduk racing towards them, with all the winds of heaven howling around him.

"Come out, Old Mother!" He taunted Tiamat.
"Leave your monsters. You and I will do battle
together!"

Tiamat came at him, in fury and frenzy, her huge
jaws wide open to swallow him. Quick as a flash
Marduk hurled his net towards Tiamat. He drove
storm winds into her gaping mouth, so that she could
not close it. Tiamat screamed and struggled furiously,
entangled in the net that imprisoned her. But it only
bound her more tightly. Now she was at the mercy of
Marduk. He took his bow and let fly an arrow into
her helpless body, piercing her to the heart. She fell,
and Marduk stood triumphant upon her lifeless body.

Tiamat's followers were filled with panic. They tried hard to run away, but the followers of Marduk surrounded them and bound them in chains. The monsters were hurled down into the darkness of the underworld where they would stay for ever.

So Marduk destroyed Tiamat, and now he could bring order to all creation. He divided Tiamat's huge body into two parts, like a man slicing a fish in half.

One half he raised up to form the arch of Sky. There he made Heaven as a home for the gods. Within the arch of Sky he set Sun and Moon and Stars. He appointed their times, their movements, and their seasons. He made a gate in the east for Sun to come through at dawn and bring the day. He made a gate in the west for Sun to pass through at dusk, bringing the night.

Marduk used the other half of Tiamat's body to make Earth. He formed mountains and hills, rivers and streams. He raised up her tail to join Sky and Earth, and to hold the arch of Heaven in place. In these ways, Marduk brought order to Earth. Now that it was shaped and watered, he created seeds and plants and animals, and the miracle of life.

Only one thing remained to be done: that was, to make Man. Marduk decided that men and women should serve the gods and provide for their needs. They were given Earth for their home and in their temples the people of Earth offered sacrifices. From their sacrifices, sweet smells rose up to bring joy to the gods.

So Marduk made the whole of creation. He appointed a great god to rule over each part: there was a Lord of the Heavens, a Lord of Earth, and a Lord of the Waters. Now all creation was in order. Now Marduk could rest from his work.

Marduk came to the assembly of all the gods in triumph, and took his seat on the throne of Heaven, his glory shining over the whole of his creation. And all the gods of Heaven, even his father, Ea, bowed low before him. "Great Lord of Creation!" was their cry.

On Earth, too, people bowed down before Marduk the Great, Marduk the Creator. In the great city of Babylon, Marduk was honoured more than in any other place, for he was the God of its people. There his praises were sung by day and night. There the sweet smell of sacrifices to Great Marduk rose up to Heaven. The Empire of Babylon grew. The fame of Marduk spread. Men worshipped many gods. But none was greater than Marduk, the God of Babylon, Creator and Lord of all.

The Sign of the Rainbow

Here is another story of the world's beginning, this
time from the Jewish religion.

*   *   *   *   *   *

When God had created the earth he filled it with life.
He made all kinds of living creatures—
birds to live in the sky, fish to live in the sea,
animals and insects to live on the land.
Then he made men and women to be his friends.
He created Adam the first man, and Eve the
first woman.
Children were born to them,
and to their children's children after them.
So the race of men and women grew, and the earth
filled with people.
They were meant to be like God,
kind and loving and good,
for God had made them in his likeness
to be his friends.
But something went wrong.
People were not kind and loving and good.
They were cruel, and hateful, and evil.

They thought up all kinds of evil in their minds.
They imagined all kinds of wrong to do with
their hands.
They were really wicked.
Then God felt sorry that he had created men
and women.
When he looked upon the earth which he had made,
he could see only one good man.
That was his servant Noah, who loved God
with all his heart.
Of all the people on earth,
only Noah was kind and loving and good.
Then God decided what he would do. He said
to himself, "I will rid the earth of people
except for Noah and his family, for I am sorry
that I ever made them.
Then I will make a fresh start on earth
with Noah and his children."
Then God spoke to Noah.
"I am going to bring a great flood on earth.
Waters will cover everything,
and all living things will die.
Only you and your family will be saved,
so that I can make a fresh start
with people who will be faithful and true to me.

This is what you must do.
Make an ark with sturdy logs from the pine trees.
It will need three storeys, a window,
and a door in the side.
Cover it with pitch, both inside and outside,
so that no water can get into it.
When the ark is finished, take into it
two of every kind of living creature,
a male and a female,
so that there can be living creatures again.
Take with you into the ark your wife,
and your three sons and their wives,
so that there can be people again.

Take a good store of food for yourselves
and for the animals, for the rains will
pour down for forty days and forty nights."
Noah did just as God had ordered.
When he had finished the ark
it was strong and sturdy and waterproof.
Then Noah went into the ark
with all his family, and with all the animals,
and sealed the door tightly.
Soon the windows of heaven opened
and the rains poured down upon the earth.
For forty days and forty nights the rains poured down.
First the low land was covered with water,
and the ark began to float.
Then the hills were covered with water,
and the ark rose higher.
Then even the high mountains were covered,
and now there was nothing but a vast sea of water.
Only Noah's ark floated safely on the mighty ocean.
All other living things had died in the floods.

★   ★   ★   ★   ★   ★

At last the rains ceased,
but it was many days before the waters
began to go down.

Then Noah opened the window of the ark.
He held out a dove in his hand and let it fly away.
He waited to see what would happen.
After some time the dove fluttered back wearily,
and Noah stretched his arm out of the window
to pull it safely into the ark.
It had found nothing on which to rest.
Seven days later Noah again sent a dove.
It was gone all day, and when it returned in the
evening, there was an olive leaf in its mouth.
So now the waters were below the tops of the trees.
Seven days later Noah sent out a dove for the
third time.
He waited and waited, but the dove never came back.

Noah knew then that the floods had gone down.
He unbarred the door of the ark
and looked out at the dry land all around.
The ark had come to rest on the mountains of Ararat.

*   *   *   *   *   *

Noah went out of the ark on to dry land,
and at once bowed down to worship God.
Then God spoke to Noah and said,
"I give my blessing to you and your sons,
and their sons after them.
Fill the earth with children.
Care for the animals and trees and plants
which I have given you for food.
Obey my laws, and follow my ways.
Be kind and loving and good.
Then I will always be your God,
and you will always be my people."
Then Noah made his solemn promise
that he and his children would always be faithful
to God,
obeying his laws and following his ways.
And God made his solemn promise to Noah,
"Never again will I cover the earth with waters.

I will watch over the earth and provide your needs.
There will always be seed-time and harvest,
cold and heat, summer and winter, day and night.
This is the sign that I will keep my promise—
I am placing a bow of many colours in the sky.
When rain clouds appear,
soon you will see my rainbow.
The rainbow will be a sign for ever of my promise
to you and to all people.''

Joseph's Secret

This story of Joseph is told in the Jewish Bible, but
it is not certain that Joseph was a real person.
There *was* famine in those days and hungry people of
other tribes had to go down to Egypt to buy corn.
But some people think that wise Jewish teachers of
long ago made up the story of Joseph's life for boys
in their schools. Joseph was a fine example for them
to follow. He became great because he used the
wisdom which God had given him to care for others.

*　　*　　*　　*　　*　　*

The people of Egypt bowed down to Joseph as he
rode by in his royal chariot. He was dressed in the
finest white linen, with a chain of gold hanging round
his neck. On his finger was the gold ring which
Pharaoh, the mighty king of Egypt, had given him.
Pharaoh had given Joseph his own ring to show that
he had made him ruler over all his land. Only
Pharaoh himself was more powerful. How proud
and important Joseph seemed as he rode by!

Yet, not long before, Joseph had been a slave
lying in prison. He had come from the land of Israel,

where his jealous brothers had got rid of him by
selling him to merchants who were on their way to
Egypt. In Egypt the merchants had sold him as a
slave to a soldier called Potiphar. In time, Potiphar
had put Joseph in charge of his whole household.
But then Potiphar's wife told lies about Joseph, and
he was thrown into prison.

Then a strange thing happened. Pharaoh had a
dream which troubled him, and he heard of how
Joseph could tell the meaning of dreams. He sent for
Joseph and told him his dream. Joseph could see
clearly what it meant. For seven years there would be
fine harvests in Egypt. Then there would be seven
years of bad harvests and hunger. Joseph told Pharaoh

that he should choose a wise man to store as much corn as possible during the good years, so that there would be enough food for the bad years.

"You are the man!" said Pharaoh. "Your God has blessed you with wisdom. You are a free man and I appoint you ruler over all my land."

The seven years of bad harvests came, and there was famine and hunger in many lands. But all through the land of Egypt there were store-houses filled with corn by the wise ruler Joseph. The people of Egypt were able to buy corn from them. Hungry people came from other lands, too, when they heard that there was corn in Egypt.

*   *   *   *   *   *

In the land of Israel the famine was great and the people were very hungry. Joseph's father, Jacob, called his sons together and said, "I hear that there is corn in Egypt. Take your asses, go down to Egypt, and buy corn for us all. I will keep young Benjamin here with me. I don't want any harm to come to him as it did to Joseph."

Jacob thought that Joseph, his favourite son, was dead, for after his brothers had sold him they had brought back his coat dipped in the blood of a goat.

So Jacob believed that Joseph had been killed by a wild beast.

When the ten brothers went down to Egypt to buy corn, they were brought before Joseph. They bowed down before the mighty ruler, and Joseph knew at once that they were his brothers. But they had no idea that the great man was the young brother they had sold as a slave. Joseph decided to keep his secret to himself. He spoke in the language of Egypt, and had his words translated into the language of his brothers. He spoke roughly to them. "Where have you come from?" he demanded.

"We have come from the land of Israel to buy corn," the brothers answered.

"You are spies!" Joseph accused them. "You have come to spy on our land!"

"No, Lord!" they answered, trembling with fear. "We are not spies. We are all brothers, sons of Jacob of Israel. Our youngest brother remained at home, and we had another brother who is dead."

"Very well," Joseph replied. "I will give you a chance to prove that you are telling the truth. One of you will stay here in prison. The rest of you can go back home and bring your youngest brother to me."

The brothers were terrified. They talked anxiously to each other, not knowing that Joseph could understand every word.

"It is a judgement on us for what we did to Joseph," they said. And as they spoke, Joseph had to turn away from them to hide the tears in his eyes. But he still kept his secret. He ordered that Simeon must stay in prison, while the rest of the brothers returned home with their sacks full of corn.

The brothers were even more troubled when they got home, for each of them found in his sack the money he had paid for the corn!

Father Jacob was bitter when they told him the whole story. "You have robbed me of my children," he cried. "First it was Joseph. Then Simeon. Now you want to take Benjamin! No, I won't let him go

with you. If anything happened to him, I would die
of a broken heart."

★   ★   ★   ★   ★   ★

The famine in Israel grew worse, and the corn the
brothers had brought back from Egypt was used up.
Then Jacob said to his sons, "You must go down to
Egypt again and buy more corn."

Judah, one of the brothers, said, "The ruler of
Egypt ordered us to bring Benjamin with us."

"Why did you tell him you had another brother?"
said Jacob angrily.

"We had to tell him everything because he thought
we were spies," Judah answered. "How could we
know that he would order us to bring Benjamin
back?" Then he pleaded with his father. "We shall
all starve to death if we don't get more corn soon,"
he said. "Let me take Benjamin, Father. I will see
that he comes to no harm. Punish me and my
family if I do not bring him back safely to you."

Then Jacob spoke with a heavy heart. "Very well,
then—but you must take presents to the ruler of
Egypt to win his favour. Take some honey, some
spices and some nuts for him. Take twice the amount
of money to pay for the corn. Take the money you

found in your sacks, too, just in case it was left there
by accident. Take Benjamin, if you must. I pray God
that the ruler of Egypt will be merciful, and let you
bring back both Simeon and Benjamin. If I lose them
I shall have nothing to live for.''

So the brothers took Benjamin with them down to
Egypt. They were terrified when Joseph's servants
took them to his own house.

''It's because of the money in our sacks,'' they
said to each other. ''The ruler's going to punish us
and make us his slaves.'' But the steward in charge of
Joseph's house spoke kindly to them. He brought
Simeon to them from prison. He had their asses led

away to be fed and watered. He treated them as guests in Joseph's house.

When Joseph came, the brothers laid their presents before him and bowed down to the ground. When he saw his dear brother Benjamin, Joseph was overcome and had to hurry away to hide his tears of joy. Then he dried his eyes and washed his face before going back to his brothers.

But still he kept his secret.

*　　*　　*　　*　　*　　*

The next morning Joseph gave strict orders to his steward. "Fill these men's sacks with as much corn as they can carry. Put each man's money inside his sack, and put my sacred silver cup in the sack of the youngest."

The steward did as Joseph ordered, and the brothers left the city to make their way home. They had not gone far when Joseph's steward galloped up to them. Joseph had told him what to say. "Why have you paid back my lord's goodness with evil?" he demanded. "You have stolen my lord's sacred silver cup!"

The brothers were amazed. "God forbid that we should do such a thing!" they cried. "If the cup is found with any of us, let him die, and let the rest of us become your lord's slaves."

"Very well," said the steward. "Open your sacks!"

The brothers gladly took their sacks off the asses, and the steward went through each one. He found the cup in Benjamin's sack. The brothers were shaking with terror as the steward's men took them back to appear before Joseph. They fell to the ground before him.

"Why have you done this to me?" Joseph said sternly.

Judah spoke for the trembling brothers. "My lord, what can we say? How can we clear ourselves? It seems that we have done this great wrong and must become your slaves."

"God forbid that I should make all of you slaves," said Joseph. "The man in whose sack the cup was found shall be my slave. The rest of you can go back to your father."

Then Judah came near to Joseph and said, "My lord, may I speak to you privately? I know you are second only to Pharaoh in this country, and I humbly beg that you will hear me. Our father Jacob had two sons in his old age and loved them dearly. One of them is no longer with him, and now he has only Benjamin—in whose sack the silver cup was found. You ordered us to bring Benjamin to you, and our father would not agree at first, for he was afraid of losing him too. He said that if anything happened to Benjamin, he would die of a broken heart. If I go back without him, our father will surely die. I pray you therefore—take me in place of Benjamin. Let me be your slave. Let Benjamin go back to bring joy to our father in his old age."

*   *   *   *   *   *

Joseph could keep his secret no longer. Quickly he ordered all his servants to go away, so that he could be alone with his brothers. Tears of joy poured down his face as he cried aloud, "I am Joseph!"

The brothers were amazed. They did not know what to think or what to say.

"Come near to me, I beg you," Joseph said to them. "I am Joseph your brother. You sold me to merchants and they brought me to Egypt. Do not feel guilty and ashamed. Do not be angry with yourselves for what you did to me. It was God who brought me to Egypt, so that I could save life in this time of famine. He has made me ruler of Egypt, second only to Pharaoh, and now I can save my own people too. Hurry back to our father and tell him that his son Joseph is ruler of Egypt. Bid him come down to dwell with me here in the land of plenty."

When Pharaoh heard the news, he was full of joy for Joseph. "Tell your brothers to bring back your father and all his family," he said. "They must take waggons for the children and old people to ride in during the journey. Your people can settle where there is good pasture for their flocks and herds, and live in plenty."

Father Jacob could not believe the amazing story that his sons brought back. But when he saw the waggons and all the gifts that Joseph had sent, he knew it must be true. "Then Joseph, my dearest son, really is alive," he said joyfully. "I must go to be with him before I die." So Jacob and his whole family, with their flocks and herds and all their possessions, went down to Egypt.

When Joseph heard that his beloved father was coming, he went eagerly to meet him. He rode in his royal chariot, dressed in the finest white linen, with a chain of gold hanging round his neck, and the ring of Pharaoh on his finger. But now he was not the proud ruler of Egypt—he was a son running to welcome his father, taking him in his arms and crying for joy.

"Now I can die in peace," Jacob said, holding Joseph to him, "for I have found you alive, my dear, dear Joseph."

The Sword of the Lord and of Gideon!

People have always admired great leaders and men
and women of courage. This story is about a great
Jewish warrior who fought, sword in hand, for his
land, his people and his God.

      ★   ★   ★   ★   ★   ★

Gideon was hard at work on his father's farm. It had
been a good harvest, and now he was busy threshing
the corn. He was beating it with a heavy stick to
separate the grains of corn from the husks and straw.

Gideon usually did this job on the flat threshing-
floor at the top of the hill, where the wind blew.
There he could toss the corn into the air with a fork,
so that the wind blew away the husks and the straw.
But now, Gideon was threshing the corn secretly in
the wine-press. The wine-press was a pit cut in the
earth where the grapes were trodden and pressed to
make wine, and it was down in the valley where
Gideon could not be seen. If he had been threshing
on the hill-top he would have been seen a long way
off. Then the Midianites would have known the corn

was ready, and they would have raided the farm to
steal it.

The Midianites were the enemies of Gideon's
people. They were wanderers who lived in the desert
and bred camels. They raided the farms of the Jews
for food and cattle and water. They came in their
hundreds, like a plague of locusts, stripping the farms
of everything, stealing and killing and destroying.
They rode furiously on their fast camels, shouting
war cries and waving their swords.

The farmers were terrified and ran for safety,
hiding in caves in the hills till the enemy had gone.
No wonder that Gideon was threshing the corn
secretly so that the Midianites would not be attracted
to his father's farm.

But Gideon was not afraid of the Midianites. He was no coward. His blood boiled as he remembered how his elder brothers had been killed in one of the enemy raids. Gideon was the youngest brother, and now he was the only son left to his father. Gideon believed that he had a sacred duty to avenge his brothers, and he longed to attack their murderers.

He thought of nothing else as he worked in the wine-press. He thought of the God of his fathers who had led his people out of Egypt and brought them into the rich land he had promised them. But since then things seemed to have gone wrong. Now, because of the Midianites, they could never work in peace. Had God forsaken his people? Why was there no leader to deliver them from the power of the Midianites?

    *   *   *   *   *   *

Then suddenly Gideon knew the answer. *He* was the leader! God was calling him to lead his people and to deliver them from the Midianites!

Gideon was on fire to start his great fight for his people. First of all, he must bring them back to the God of their fathers. They had begun to worship the gods of this new land. Now that the people of Israel

44

were farmers, they worshipped the gods who were supposed to rule over the earth, and to give good crops to their worshippers.

The chief of these gods was Baal, and the people of Gideon's town had built an altar to him and to his Goddess. There they went to worship, and to pray for a good harvest on their land.

That very night, Gideon went out secretly with loyal servants and he smashed the altar to pieces. The men of the town were furious when they saw that the altar had been destroyed.

"Who has done this evil?" they cried. "He must die!" When they found out that it was Gideon, they went in a crowd to the farmhouse.

"Bring out your son!" they yelled to Gideon's father. "He must die for his crime against Baal!"

The old farmer came out and faced them. "Are you standing up for Baal?" he said, scornfully. "Does he need you for his champions? Let Baal stand up for himself! If he really is a God, let him destroy Gideon himself!"

Then the men were ashamed and slunk away, for they knew they were betraying the God of their fathers when they worshipped other gods.

*   *   *   *   *   *

Now Gideon sent messengers round to the other tribes. He called them to join him and to fight for their God and their country. They were to meet Gideon in the hills. From there they could look down on the valley of Jezreel, where a great army of Midianites had pitched their tents.

Men came to Gideon from far and near, and when they were counted he found that he had thirty-two thousand men! They were much too many for Gideon. He was far too clever to want a great battle between the two armies. His plans were simple and daring. He was going to defeat the Midianites by cunning, and he needed only a small band of brave men.

So he spoke hard words to the men around him. "Look! Down there, in the valley, you can see the great army you must fight! The Midianites are strong! The battle will be hard! You will face danger and death! If anyone's afraid, let him go back home!"

Many of the men were glad when they heard this. They were terrified of the Midianites, and thousands went back home. This left ten thousand men to fight, but still there were far too many for Gideon. So he decided he would test them to find out who would make the best warriors. "Come down to the river!" he cried. "Let us drink well before we go into battle!"

When they reached the river bank, many men went down on their knees to drink, dipping their faces in the water. They could not see around them, so they could easily be surprised and attacked. No true warrior would be so careless, making himself helpless while he was drinking.

Then Gideon saw that three hundred men used their hands like a cup and lifted the water to their mouths. They could still see all around them. They were watchful and alert. These three hundred were the men for Gideon, and he sent the rest back home.

* * * * * *

Gideon was a fine warrior. He planned to take the enemy by surprise. He was going to attack the Midianites in the dark of night, while they slept. He divided his men into three companies of one hundred men each, so that they could attack the camp from different sides. Then the Midianites would think they were being attacked by a huge army all around the camp.

Gideon prepared his men. Each one had a sword, and a horn for sounding the battle-cry. Each man had a big jug made of baked clay, with a lighted lamp hidden inside it. The signal for the attack was to be

given by Gideon with a blast on his horn.

At dead of night, the three hundred men crept
silently through the darkness. They took up their
positions around the camp of the sleeping Midianites.
When they were all ready, Gideon blew his horn. At
once his men sounded their horns all round the camp.
They smashed their jugs, held their lamps up for
light, and burst into the camp shouting their battle-
cry—"The Sword of the Lord and of Gideon!"

The sleeping Midianites were suddenly woken by
the terrible noise all around them. It must be a huge
army attacking them! They seized their swords and
leapt up to defend themselves. In the darkness and
confusion they could not tell friend from enemy, and
many attacked each other. They fled in panic, with
Gideon's three hundred warriors hot on their heels.

They chased the Midianites back to the River
Jordan. Men from other tribes helped Gideon by
taking prisoners. Finally, Gideon and his men caught
up with the last of the enemy. Among them were their
two leaders. They were sheikhs of the desert, with
gold rings in their ears, and gold chains hanging over
their purple robes. Their camels too had golden
chains around their necks, decorated with ornaments
shaped like the moon.

Gideon asked the sheikhs to tell him about the raid
in which his brothers had been killed. Then he said,
"The men you killed were my brothers. If you had
spared their lives, then I would have spared yours.
But you killed them—you killed all my brothers."
So Gideon slew the two princes of Midian. At last
he had avenged his brothers, and his sacred duty had
been done.

The few Midianites who survived the battle went back to the desert of Arabia with the terrible tidings. Never again did the Midianites come against the land of Israel.

*　　*　　*　　*　　*　　*

When Gideon came back he was a popular hero among his own people. Men of other tribes, too, had seen what a fine leader he was, and how he had brought the tribes together to save their land. They came to Gideon and said, "You have led us to victory in battle. Lead us now as our king! Rule over us— you and your children after you!"

But Gideon replied, "No! I will not be your king! I will not rule over you—nor my children after me. God is your king! He will rule over you!"

Gideon went back to his own village, back to his family, his farm, his herds and his fields. There he lived to be a good old age, and there he was buried with his fathers. But he was never forgotten, and we can still read in the Jewish Bible the story of Gideon the warrior with his battle-cry, "The Sword of the Lord and of Gideon!"

Holy Places: Synagogue

Long ago, when the Jews were conquered and taken away from Israel, they could no longer worship God in their temple at Jerusalem. Instead, they met and worshipped God in a synagogue. The word "synagogue" means "meeting together", and still today Jews meet and worship together in their synagogues. They worship God with psalms, prayers, readings from their Bible, and a sermon. Even a small number of Jews who wish to seek God through prayer and study may start a synagogue, wherever they live, and look after it themselves.

So a synagogue can often be quite a simple building. The most holy part is a cupboard on the

east wall, facing towards the Holy City of Jerusalem,
where the Jews' temple once stood. This holy
cupboard is called the Ark, and inside it are the
precious Scrolls of the Law of Moses. A light that
burns day and night in front of the Ark is a sign of
God's presence, and reminds Jews of the lights that
once shone in the temple at Jerusalem. When the
Scrolls are carried through the synagogue for reading
during the service, everyone bows towards them.
The Ark, and the fine velvet wrappings of the
Scrolls, are often decorated with the star of David,
the special sign of the Jewish people.

An Unexpected Treasure

In many countries stories are told of hardworking
men whose sons turn out to be either lazy or greedy.
Often such stories have a twist at the end—like this
one. It is a parable of the Moslem people who follow
the religion of Islam.

★   ★   ★   ★   ★   ★

Long ago, in a land of the East, there lived a farmer
named Abdullah. He had worked hard all his life,
and now he was a rich man with a fine farm and four
large fields.

Everyone knew Farmer Abdullah and respected
him, for he was a good man. He loved to help anyone
in need, and he gave much of his money to the poor.
Everyone praised the kind and generous farmer, but
secretly they felt sorry for him too, for he had three
lazy sons. Their names were Hussein, Ahmad and
Hakim.

Hussein spent his time in feasting and dancing.
Ahmad was busy racing horses, and Hakim liked
sword-fighting. The three brothers were far too busy
enjoying themselves to help their father with his
work on the farm. In fact, not one of them had ever

done a day's work in his life. No wonder that people felt sorry for Farmer Abdullah, with his three worthless sons wasting his hard-earned money instead of working to earn their own livings.

"Why should we work?" said Hussein to his brothers. "Father's got plenty of money."

"And when he dies, we'll have his treasure to live on," said Ahmad.

"And we can hire men to work on the farm for us," added Hakim.

So the three lazy sons of Farmer Abdullah went on enjoying themselves, sure that they would never have to work.

The time came when old Farmer Abdullah lay dying. He sent for his three sons and they stood by his bed.

"I am leaving my farm to all three of you," he said. "You will find my treasure buried in the first field." And with that, the old man died.

The three greedy brothers could hardly wait to get their hands on their father's fortune.

"Come on!" said Hussein. "Let's start digging. We'll soon find it."

So the three brothers set to work. They went to the field next to the farm and started digging. They were not used to hard work and they soon had sore hands and aching backs. The sweat poured off them, but the brothers went on digging cheerfully, for at any moment they expected to find the treasure chest.

First they dug all the way across the field, then they dug all the way down the field. Day after day they went on digging, and it was not long before they had dug the whole field. But they did not find the treasure. Where could it be?

✶   ✶   ✶   ✶   ✶   ✶

"Perhaps we've been digging the wrong field," said Hussein. "After all, we don't really know what father meant by the 'first' field."

"Perhaps he made a mistake," said Ahmad, "and forgot which field he had put the treasure in."

There was nothing for it but to start digging the next field.

"Wait a minute," said Hakim. "I've got an idea. Now that we've dug up all this field, let's sow some seed in it. Then we could sell the crop and make some money."

So the brothers planted wheat in the field they had dug, before starting work on the next one. Then they dug all over the second field, but there was no treasure there either. So again they planted wheat. Then they dug up the third field—but again they found no treasure. Now there was only one field left. The treasure simply *had* to be there.

Full of hope, the brothers dug all over the last field, but still they found no treasure. They planted it with wheat and went back to the farmhouse. They were angry and bitter after all their hard work.

"Our father has cheated us!" cried Hussein.

"He must have given all his treasure away!" said Ahmad angrily. "What a fool he was!"

"How could he treat his own sons like this!" said Hakim bitterly.

But it was not long before they had to be busy working again. Huge crops of wheat had grown up in the four fields that they had dug so well. Now it was ready for harvesting. The three brothers could not help feeling rather proud of themselves as they took their fine crop to sell at the market. They made so

much more money than they had expected, that they returned home feeling a good deal happier.

*   *   *   *   *   *

Now the fields were bare and empty again, and still the three brothers could not forget the treasure that their father had promised them.

"Perhaps we didn't dig deep enough," said Hussein. "We might have missed the treasure the first time. Let's dig the fields again to make sure."

"We might as well," said Ahmad. "After all, we're quite used to digging by now—and we're getting quite good at it."

"We could sow wheat again too," said Hakim. "Then our digging wouldn't be wasted, and we'd make good money as well."

So, once again, the three brothers dug up the four fields, still hoping to find their father's treasure. They did not find it, but, as before, they planted wheat. Again they had a fine harvest and made a lot of money from their crop. They went on like that, year after year, still hoping to find their father's treasure. They grew used to hard work and became good farmers and rich men. They grew all kinds of crops and made a lot of money. All the people who knew them were puzzled. They just could not understand

why those lazy and worthless sons of Farmer Abdullah
had grown into honest, hardworking farmers.

*　　*　　*　　*　　*　　*

One day the brothers were talking together.

"You know, I think our father was very clever,"
said Hussein.

"Why?" asked Ahmad.

"He knew that there was no treasure hidden in his
fields. He just told us that because he knew how
greedy we were. He knew that we would dig up every
piece of his land to get our hands on his treasure.
He knew, too, that we would sow seed rather than
waste all our digging. That was how he turned us
into real hardworking farmers!"

"So his treasure was really all the money that we
have made from farming," said Ahmad.

"It was more than that," said Hakim. "We only
made that money by working hard. And we only
worked hard because we were greedy. Father used
our greed to turn us into good farmers. Now we
know the value of hard work and of earning our own
livings. That was the *real* treasure that we found
in father's fields."

Holy Places: Mosque

Moslems bow down with their faces to the ground when they pray to Allah. Mosque, the name of their building for meeting and worship, means a place for bowing down. A mosque, built with bricks or stones, is a square building around an open courtyard. At the front, or at the corners, there are towers called minarets. From the minarets, a Moslem calls people to the prayers which must be said five times each day.

Mosques are built so that the worshippers are facing towards the Holy City of Mecca as they pray.

Moslems wash their faces and hands and feet before praying, and leave their shoes outside the mosque. Prayers can be said anywhere—but always facing towards the Holy City of Mecca.

Judging Others

When Jesus was teaching the people about God he told them stories about everyday life, to help them understand what he really meant. By thinking about these stories they began to see the meaning of his words. Stories like these are called parables. This is one of the parables of Jesus which are treasured by his followers who are called Christians.

*   *   *   *   *   *

There were once two brothers whose names were Peter and John. They were carpenters, so they spent their days working with wood. They had a fine workshop, with all the tools they needed, and plenty of wood of all shapes and sizes. They enjoyed their work, and often sang as they sawed up the long planks into smaller pieces of wood for making things. There was always a lot of sawdust in their workshop—on the bench, on the floor, and even in the air.

One morning Peter looked hard at John. "Why, John," he said, "I can see a speck of sawdust in your eye. Here, let me get it out for you."

Peter set to work with his fingers, trying to get the

tiny speck of dust out of John's eye. He worked
clumsily, for his fingers were thick and hard from his
woodwork. It took him a long time, but he would not
give up. He fumbled away with his fingers till at last
he got it out.

"It's out!" he cried triumphantly. "There, now
you can see again!"

Peter felt very pleased with himself. Not only had
he noticed the tiny speck of dust in John's eye, but
he had managed to get it out, too!

But something else was wrong. Peter had something
in *his* eye as well. But it was no speck of dust this
time. It was much bigger than that. It was a great
big plank! It was sticking out of Peter's eye for
everyone to see. And Peter had not even noticed it!

How people must have laughed when Jesus told this parable! But it was not just a funny story—it was telling something about all of us. Peter had been so busy finding something wrong with John that he had not even noticed that there was something wrong with himself. And it was much, much bigger!

Jesus was really saying, get rid of your own big faults first. Then you will be able to see more clearly. Then you will see how tiny the faults of others are, and how big yours are. And if you don't like other people finding fault with you, don't find fault with them!

Paul the Prisoner

In the days of the Romans, going by sea was one of the most dangerous ways to travel in winter, and shipwrecks were common. When Paul, one of the first Christians, was shipwrecked he had with him a loyal friend called Luke, who was a Greek doctor. Luke kept a diary, and in it he wrote down the full story of what happened. This story is in the Christian Bible and you can still read it today.

*   *   *   *   *   *

For two long years Paul had been a prisoner at Caesarea, a Roman town on the coast of Israel. Before that, he had been a missionary for over twenty years, spreading the Good News of Jesus. He had travelled far and wide setting up Christian churches. He had made many friends, but he had made enemies too. Some Jews hated Paul for preaching that Jesus was the Saviour sent by God to his people. They had stirred up a riot in which Paul was arrested, and now he was waiting to be tried by the Romans.

As soon as a new Roman Governor was appointed, Paul was brought before him to be tried. Paul's

Jewish enemies had come from Jerusalem, and they made all kinds of charges against him.

Paul defended himself. "I have not broken the Laws of the Jews," he said to the Governor. "I have not broken the Laws of the Romans. I have done no wrong. I claim justice from you."

The new Governor wanted to be just and fair. "Are you willing to go to Jerusalem so that I can try your case before the Council of the Jews?" he asked Paul.

But Paul knew that in Jerusalem his enemies would stir up the Council against him. He had no hope of getting justice in Israel—his enemies would see to that! But, since Paul was a citizen of the Roman Empire, he had the right to be tried by the great

Emperor of Rome, Caesar himself. Paul claimed that right. "I am a freeborn Roman citizen," he said to the Governor. "I appeal to Caesar!"

"Very well," replied the Governor. "You have appealed to Caesar. You shall go to Caesar."

*   *   *   *   *   *

To go before Caesar, Paul had to be taken to Rome. He would have to sail by ship across the Mediterranean Sea, and a Roman officer named Julius was put in charge of him to see that he got to Rome safely.

Paul was an important prisoner and Julius treated him well. He allowed Paul to take two friends with him as his servants. One of them was Luke, a Greek doctor who had become a Christian and travelled everywhere with Paul. Luke kept a diary of their travels, and later he used his diary to write a history book about the early Christians.

It was now the end of summer. In autumn, the Mediterranean Sea became rough and dangerous, making sailing difficult. As winter storms approached, sailing stopped altogether. Julius knew there was no time to waste. Few ships sailed straight from Caesarea to Rome, so he decided to take a small ship sailing northwards. He would be able to get a ship to Rome from one of the bigger ports up the coast. So Julius and his soldiers took Paul on to the coastal ship. There were some other prisoners too, but they had already been tried and condemned. They were to die when they reached Rome.

★   ★   ★   ★   ★   ★

The little ship sailed along the coast till, after fifteen days, it reached the busy port of Myra. There Julius found a ship that was sailing to Italy, and took his prisoners on board.

The ship was carrying wheat from North Africa to provide bread for the great city of Rome. Grain ships like this sailed even in dangerous weather, because their cargoes were so important. It was quite a big ship, for altogether there were nearly three hundred people on board, as well as the cargo of wheat.

In Roman times, sailors had no compasses to help them to steer their ships. Instead, they used the sun by day and the stars by night to guide them on their journeys. So on a cloudy night they had no way of knowing where they were. Even big ships were helpless in a storm. No wonder that sailors tried to

avoid rough waters and stormy weather whenever
they could!

The ship sailed south to the large island of Crete.
There it took shelter in the Bay of Fair Havens on
the south side of the island, where it was protected
by the land from the dangerous north winds. It stayed
there for some days, safe from bad weather.

But it was now late September and the stormy
season was near. Since Julius was in charge, as chief
officer on the ship, he had to decide what to do.
Paul knew all about the dangers of the sea from his
travels, and he advised Julius to stay where they were
for the winter.

The owner of the ship and his captain, however, thought it would be better to spend the winter in a safer harbour, seventy kilometres to the west. Julius decided to take *their* advice. The ship set sail westwards—but it never reached the harbour.

* * * * * *

At first there was a pleasant wind blowing from the south. Then suddenly a fierce north-easterly blew up, sweeping down from the mountains of Crete. The ship, with just one main-sail, could only run before the gale. But it was blown close to a little island, where the wind dropped for a while. There the sailors were able to pass ropes around the ship to hold the planks together. This would help to save it from sinking, for if the wheat got wet it would swell and burst the planks apart.

There was another danger they all knew about. If the ship ran before the north-east gale for long, it could be blown on to the dreaded quicksands off the coast of North Africa. Many ships had been sucked into them. The only answer was to lower the main-sail, leaving just enough to try to steer the ship to the west. They did this, but the thick storm clouds hid the stars. The sailors had nothing to guide them, and the helpless ship was tossed about by the angry seas.

That night, Paul dreamed that he had arrived safely at Rome and appeared before Caesar. In his dream, the ship had been wrecked on an island, but no one on board had been lost. In those days, men believed that dreams told of things which would happen in the future. So Paul's dream was good news, and the others were cheered by it when he told them.

*　　*　　*　　*　　*　　*

For fourteen days and nights the ship was at the mercy of the raging storm. Then, at midnight, the sailors found that the water was less deep and they knew that land was near. They dropped four anchors to keep the ship off any rocks. The anchors were lowered from the stern so that the front of the ship would be facing land. That would make it easier to run the ship ashore. Now they had to wait for daylight. But some of the crew could think only of saving their own skins. They began to lower the ship's boat, pretending that they were lowering more anchors. Paul saw their trickery and told Julius. He knew that without the crew to man the ship, everyone would be in danger when they tried to

beach it. At once Julius ordered his men to cut the ropes so that the boat floated away.

Again Paul showed what a good leader he was. He advised everyone to eat while they waited for daylight. This would give them strength for the struggle to get the ship ashore. Paul ate some food himself, and the rest followed his example. The cargo of wheat was thrown overboard to lighten the ship for driving ashore.

When daylight came, they could see a creek, and decided to aim for it. The anchors were raised and the main-sail was hoisted. The wind blew the ship towards the shore, as they had hoped, but it ran aground just off the land, and the waves began to pound and smash the helpless vessel. The soldiers wanted to kill the prisoners, so that none of them could escape by swimming off. But Julius stopped

them, for he wanted to save Paul. He ordered all those who could swim to make for the shore. The rest followed on planks from the broken ship. So everyone on board came ashore safely—just as Paul's dream had foretold.

*   *   *   *   *   *

The ship had been wrecked off an island called Melita. The name came from the Greek word for honey, for which the island was famous. Today this name has become "Malta", and the place where Paul's ship was wrecked is still called St Paul's Bay.

By now it was November, cold and damp, but the people on the island were kind and helpful. They soon provided warmth and food and shelter for the passengers and crew of the ship. The chief man of the island, Publius, took Paul and his friends into his own home. The father of Publius was ill with a fever. Paul prayed over him, laid hands on him, and healed him. Then many more islanders came to Paul, bringing their sick to be healed.

After three months, the better weather came and it was possible to sail again. Another grain ship had spent the winter at Malta, and Julius decided to take his prisoners on it for the journey to Rome. A south wind carried the ship to the island of Sicily. From there, it was a smooth trip to the busy and bustling port of Puteoli, near the city of Naples. Now they were on the mainland of Italy, and a fine road led to the great city of Rome, 230 kilometres away.

There were some Christians at the port of Puteoli, and Paul was able to spend a few days with them. There were Christians at other places too. They

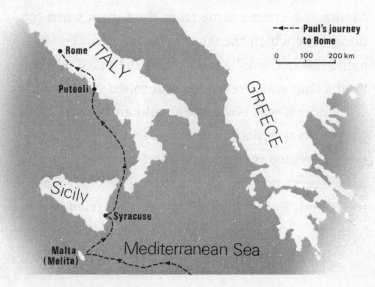

came to greet Paul as he followed the road to Rome with Julius and his soldiers. That road is still there today, part of it just as it was in the time of Paul.

*   *   *   *   *   *

So, at last, Paul arrived at Rome, and there Doctor Luke's diary ended. He had told the story of how news of Jesus and his teaching had come from faraway Jerusalem to the city of Rome. His story finished by saying that Paul had to wait for two years to be tried before Caesar, the Emperor of Rome.

Paul made good use of those two years. He wrote many letters, which we can still read today. Messengers came from churches he had set up in different places, and they took Paul's letters back with them.

Paul knew that he had not long to live. "I have fought a good fight," he wrote. "I have kept faithful to Jesus. Now I am ready to go and live with him for ever."

Other Christian writers told how Paul was put to death in Rome by the Emperor Nero. But Paul's life and teaching will never be forgotten, for through his faith and courage Christianity had spread throughout the Roman Empire.

Holy Places: Church

The most common name for the building in which Christians meet to worship their Lord Jesus is "church". Important towns and cities sometimes have a "cathedral" as well.

The most holy part is the east end which faces towards the Holy Land of Israel, where Jesus lived. Here, at the east end of the church, there is a holy table called an altar, which is used for worship.

Other names for the place where Christians meet are the "Lord's House", "chapel", "meeting-house" and "citadel". These buildings are different because not all Christians worship the Lord Jesus in the same way. Some Christians follow set forms of service laid down hundreds of years ago. Others prefer to be free to worship the Lord Jesus in any way they choose.

Most Christians meet together to worship as a congregation: they sing hymns and psalms, they pray together, parts of the Bible are read aloud, and sometimes a sermon is given. But however differently they worship, all Christians meet together at their Lord's House for the same reason—to show their love for God and for their Lord Jesus, and to learn how to serve him.

Antelope, Woodpecker and Turtle

In lands of the East, millions of people follow the teachings of Lord Buddha, the Wise One. They are called Buddhists. Buddha lived in India long, long ago, but people still follow his wise teachings, which are known as The Path.

One of the things Buddha taught was that each person has many lives, not just one life, and may have lived on earth before, either as a human being or as an animal.

Buddha said that he himself had lived on earth many times before he came as the Wise One. Buddhists love to hear the stories about Buddha's different lives. They are called "Jataka" stories, for in India "Jataka" means "birth". Here is a Jataka story of how Buddha had once been born on earth as an animal—an antelope.

★　　★　　★　　★　　★　　★

When Buddha lived on earth as an antelope, his home was in a thick forest. Every morning he came out of the forest to drink at the lovely lake near by. That was how he made friends with Woodpecker, who had his home in the hole of a tree by the lake. When Antelope arrived for his morning drink, Woodpecker would stop pecking away for insects and fly down for a chat.

Someone else lived near the lake too. It was Turtle. Turtle carried his home on his back, so he never felt like travelling very far from the lake. He was always there when Antelope and Woodpecker met for their morning chat, and soon made friends with them. So now there were three friends— Antelope, Woodpecker and Turtle—who met each day to enjoy each other's company.

★　　★　　★　　★　　★　　★

One day, something happened that brought them even closer together and made their friendship stronger than ever. Danger threatened all three of them. It came from a hunter who lived in the village on the other side of the lake.

That morning, antelope came down to drink at the lake as usual, when suddenly he let out a cry of pain and terror. At once Woodpecker swooped down from his tree, and Turtle plodded up as fast as he could. They soon saw what had happened to their friend Antelope. He had trodden on a trap laid there by the hunter, and his foot was held fast.

There was no time to lose, for sooner or later the hunter would come round to see if he had caught any animals in his traps. Somehow, Woodpecker and Turtle had to save their friend Antelope.

"I know!" said Woodpecker briskly, after

examining the trap. "You set to work on those straps, friend Turtle, for they hold the trap together. We know you have no teeth, so you'll just have to use your jaws. If you can gnaw through those straps our friend Antelope will be freed. I'll go to the village and pay a call on Master Hunter. I'll keep him busy, to give you plenty of time." Then Woodpecker went on cheerfully, "Don't you worry, friend Antelope, we'll soon have you out of that cruel trap!"

So Turtle set to work on the leather straps, and Woodpecker flew off to the village as fast as he could.

★　　★　　★　　★　　★　　★

Woodpecker reached the village just in time, for the hunter was leaving his house to go round and see what animals he had caught in his traps. Woodpecker let out a shrill whistle and dived straight into the hunter's face.

Now everyone in the village knew that birds like Woodpecker brought bad luck. "It's a bad sign," said the hunter to himself. "If I go round to inspect the traps today, something dreadful will happen to me. I'd better not risk it." So he went back into his house and shut the door.

But Woodpecker was a wise old bird. "I know

what Master Hunter will do!" he said to himself. "As soon as he's got over the shock, he'll think how stupid he is to stay at home, just because of what people say about woodpeckers. Then he'll come out through the back door, because I might be still here at the front." So Woodpecker went round to the back of the house and waited.

Sure enough, out came the hunter. Again Woodpecker let out a shrill whistle, and again he dived straight into the man's face. The frightened hunter hurried back indoors. Two bad signs were enough! He stayed indoors for the rest of the day

while Woodpecker kept guard from a nearby tree.

Next morning, as soon as it was light, the hunter came hurrying out to go round his traps to see if he had caught any animals.

"I can't hope to frighten him again," thought Woodpecker, and he hurried back to the lake to warn his friends.

★   ★   ★   ★   ★   ★

"Master Hunter's coming!" cried Woodpecker, as he swooped down to his two friends by the lake. "Hurry up, friend Turtle!" he said anxiously, seeing that Turtle was still gnawing at a strap.

Poor Turtle was quite worn out. He had not stopped since Woodpecker had left the day before. His mouth was bleeding, and he could hardly move his jaws, but now he had the last strap in his mouth. Woodpecker tried hard to help by pecking desperately at the tough leather.

Then out of the wood came the hunter, his knife ready in his hand. Somehow, the two friends broke the last strap just in time. Antelope, free at last, made off on three legs to the forest. Woodpecker flew up into his tree. But poor Turtle just flopped on the ground, exhausted.

"He'll do," said the hunter, picking up Turtle and dumping him in his empty sack.

*   *   *   *   *   *

As Antelope reached the edge of the forest, and the safety of the trees, he looked back just in time to see Turtle disappearing into the hunter's sack.

At once Antelope turned round and hurried back to save his friend Turtle. He pretended to be worn out so that the hunter would think he was an easy catch. Then the cruel hunter dropped his sack and came after Antelope with his knife, licking his lips at the thought of all the fine meat he would have. Antelope kept just out of his reach, skipping away and leading him a merry dance into the forest. Deeper and deeper he went till the hunter was quite lost.

But Antelope knew every track through the trees and he raced back to his friend Turtle, still caught in the sack.

Now it was Antelope's turn to save his friend. He used his horns to undo the sack so that Turtle could be free. Turtle emerged from the dark, smelly sack just as Woodpecker swooped down from his tree. How happy the three friends were to be safe and free again!

"But we mustn't stay here," Antelope warned his friends. "Master Hunter is bound to be back before long. We must each find a safe place to hide."

So Woodpecker flew back into his tree, Antelope bounded off into the forest, and Turtle plodded into the lake. When the hunter found his way back, his sack was empty. There was no sign of Antelope or Woodpecker or Turtle. There was nothing for it but to go back home, with nothing to show for all his hunting.

Next morning the three friends met at the lake just
the same as usual, though keeping their eyes open for
any traps. Somehow, they felt much closer to each
other and they knew now that there was nothing
stronger than friendship. They had proved it by
facing danger together, and the three animals stayed
close friends for the rest of their lives.

★　　★　　★　　★　　★　　★

When Buddha told his followers this story of his life
as an antelope, they knew it was really a lesson about
friendship. "How strong we three friends were when
we faced danger together!" said Buddha. "There is
nothing stronger than the love of true friends for
each other."

Holy Places: Pagoda

Pagodas are the holy places of Buddhists, and the first ones were built over the remains of Lord Buddha or of one of his disciples. A pagoda, wherever it is built, brings happiness and prosperity to the district. In India and Ceylon, the pagodas were shaped like bells. In China and Japan, they were built in storeys, like the houses. Each storey is the same shape, but slightly smaller than the one below, and has an ornamental roof which sticks out. But every pagoda has a wide bottom, which stands for Earth, and rises up to a thin spire, which stands for the wisdom of Lord Buddha.

Inside a pagoda there are statues of Buddha. Here, Buddhists make their offerings and say their prayers. Around the outside of a pagoda there are tiny bells which tinkle in the wind. Buddhists passing by hear their gentle sound. It makes them think about their pagoda, and it reminds them of their Lord Buddha.

Guru Nanak

The Sikhs of India have always been travellers. When Britain ruled over India, many of them joined the British Army and went to other lands. Sikhs came to Britain to study or to work, and many Sikhs have made their home in Britain. Wherever they live, they follow the customs of their people, and you will always know a Sikh by the turban round his head. This story tells of the beginning of their religion, and of the Sikh holy book.

*   *   *   *   *   *

Long ago, in the country of India, there lived a man named Nanak. His home was in the Punjab, which means "Land of Five Streams". His people were Hindus who worshipped the Gods and Goddesses of India. Hindus believed that everyone was born into a certain class or group. These groups were called *castes*. Nanak was born into a high class of Hindu.

Now the land of Punjab had been conquered by people known as Moslems who followed another religion called Islam. They called God "Allah", and they believed that he was the only God. So because

Hindus and Moslems believed such different things, it was not easy for them to live together. They often became enemies and fought each other.

Nanak worked for the Moslem prince who governed his country, so he knew as much about the religion of Moslems as he did about his own. He hated fighting, and longed to know how people could live together in peace. And more than anything else, he longed to find the truth about God.

One day, Nanak went to the sacred river to bathe. Hindus believed that their lives were made pure and free from evil if they washed in the holy waters. Nanak took off his clothes and left them with his servant. Then he went deep into the waters, and his servant lost sight of him.

After some time, the servant grew anxious and hurried to the town to tell the Governor. The Governor ordered his men to search the river, but they found no trace of Nanak. Everyone believed that he had drowned.

Then after three days, Nanak appeared again at the very place where he had gone into the river. He did not say what had happened to him. He just said, "There is no Hindu. There is no Moslem." And everyone wondered, "What does he mean?"

While he was in the sacred river, Nanak had seen a
vision of God. Now he knew how men could live
together in peace. God had sent him to teach men
the truth. So Nanak left his home and became a
Guru—a Teacher of Truth. "God is the Father of all
mankind," said Guru Nanak. "All men are brothers."

This meant that there were no Hindus and no
Moslems. It meant that there were no Hindu classes,
dividing one Hindu from another. It meant that men
were not more important than women, as Hindus
believed. "See the light of God in everyone," said
Guru Nanak, "and live together as brothers."

He went to the holy places of Hindus and Moslems
to teach men about God. "There is only one God,"

said Guru Nanak. "Eternal Truth is his name. He is the Creator of all things." Nanak taught men how to live when they believed in the one true God. Since God is Eternal Truth, his followers must be true to one another. Telling lies is a wrong against God, as well as a wrong against other people. God lives in a good man, and makes him pure in all his ways. But simply bathing in the sacred river did not make a man pure. "A thief is still a thief," said Guru Nanak, "even if he does bathe in holy waters."

Many of the things that Guru Nanak taught seemed quite wrong to both the Hindus and the Moslems. People were angered by his new teachings. But some Hindus and Moslems came to believe in his teaching because they too wanted to find the truth about God. They became his followers and were called *Sikhs,* which means disciples.

Guru Nanak set up a home where his disciples lived together as brothers. They worked together and prayed together. Most important of all, they ate together. This went against the rule that Hindus could eat only with people from their own class. The disciples of Nanak came from all classes of Hindus and, of course, some were Moslems. Hindus and Moslems could never eat together, so by eating and drinking together, Sikhs proved that they were brothers.

The disciples of Nanak had one room made into a temple to say their prayers. This temple was called a *gurdwara*. There was a separate room for eating together. Guru Nanak called it the "temple of eating", for by eating together as brothers, the Sikhs were showing their faith in God. But Sikhs believed that *all* men were their brothers, so the "temple of eating" was open to everyone—especially to those who were poor and needy.

         *   *   *   *   *   *

When Guru Nanak grew old, he chose his closest disciple to be Guru after him. This second Guru wrote down the hymns which Nanak had taught to his Sikhs. They were written in the language called Punjabi, which Sikhs spoke with each other. Now every Sikh would be able to read the teachings of Guru Nanak.

Many people could not read and write, however, so Sikhs set up their own schools. There children could learn to read the hymns of Nanak, and to live by his teachings.

Just as Nanak had chosen the Guru to follow him,

so the next Guru did the same. Sikhs had ten Gurus, one after the other. Each Guru was chosen by the one before, and each Guru believed that God spoke through him. So the teachings of Guru Nanak spread, and more and more people became Sikhs.

Some people came to hate the Sikhs as they grew in number. Sikhs were attacked because their beliefs were so different from others. Two of the Gurus were even put to death. The tenth Guru decided that Sikhs must defend themselves, and he formed them into a brotherhood of men who were ready to die for their faith. They swore to keep five customs:

They would not cut their hair or shave their beards.
They would wear a comb to keep their long hair in place.
They would wear shorts, so that they could move quickly in battle.
They would wear a steel bracelet on their right wrist.
They would carry a short sword.
All the men also wore turbans, wound round their heads, and beards to show that they belonged to the brotherhood of Sikhs. They all

added the word *Singh* (which means lion) to
their names, and the women added the name
Kaur (which means princess).

★   ★   ★   ★   ★   ★

The tenth Guru who gave the Sikhs these customs
was also the last Guru. He did not choose a disciple
to follow him. Instead, he gave Sikhs a Guru that
would be with them for ever.

Sikhs had always treasured the hymns of Guru
Nanak, written for them in their own language of
Punjabi. Other writings had been added to them, and
the sacred writings of Sikhs grew into a holy book.
It was called the *Granth*. The tenth Guru completed
the Granth, and now it was a book of nearly 5 900

hymns. Before he died, he said to his people, "I am not going to choose a Guru to follow me, for now you have a Guru that will always be with you. It is the Guru Granth Sahib—the Lord Teacher Book. God speaks to you through this holy book, just as he spoke through Nanak and the other Gurus. Honour the Lord Teacher Book as your living Guru."

*   *   *   *   *   *

Wherever they live, Sikhs meet together to worship God in their gurdwara. The Granth is a very important part of that worship and when it is brought into the gurdwara, every Sikh bows towards it. It is placed on a stand called the throne, for the Sikhs honour it as though it were their living Guru speaking to them. Readings from it remind Sikhs of the truth about God, and of how they should live together as brothers.

The Lord Teacher Book is the centre of their temple. It is the centre of their homes too, for in every home, Sikhs have a special place for the Granth. The family gathers together to hear the words of the living Guru. There they hear the words of Guru Nanak who taught that God is Father of all, and that Sikhs should live as brothers of all.

Holy Places: Gurdwara

Wherever Sikhs live, they meet together and worship God in their temple. It is called a gurdwara, and the most famous is the beautiful Golden Temple at Amritsar, in India—the Holy City of the Sikhs.

But the gurdwara may be just a simple house or hall. The most holy part is the platform at the front on which rests the Granth, the holy book of Sikhs. The platform has a decorated canopy over it.

Sikhs believe that God speaks to them through the Granth, and everyone bows down to honour the holy book when it is brought in for the service. Every home has a special place too, where the family meet to hear the words of their holy book.

When Sikhs meet at their gurdwara, they go to be with their friends as well as to take part in the service and say their prayers together. Someone may give a talk or sing a hymn, accompanied by music, for the Sikhs have no special ministers to lead their worship. The service ends with everyone sharing a special food, eating together as the Sikhs have always done.

The most important festival of Sikhs is in November when they celebrate the birthday of Guru Nanak, the founder of their faith.

The Largest Family in the World

Christians show their love for God by caring for
others. This story is about Doctor Barnardo, who
spent his whole life caring for homeless children.
The work that he began many years ago is still
carried on today by people who believe, as he did,
that caring for others is part of being a Christian.

*　　*　　*　　*　　*　　*

Thomas Barnardo grew up in the city of Dublin
in Ireland. When he left school he went to work in an
office, but the job did not satisfy him and he was not
happy there. Thomas Barnardo was a Christian. He
believed all that Jesus had taught about God's love
and the need to care for others. So each evening,
after work, he went to the slums where poor people
lived, and spent his spare time helping them.

One evening, he heard a famous missionary talk
about the work he did in China, where he had gone to
teach the people about Jesus. That very night,
Thomas Barnardo felt deep inside him that he, too,

must go to China as a missionary. He knew, however, that first he had to prepare himself. He decided that the best way to show people how much God loved them would be by healing the sick.

So he left Ireland and went to London to study to become a doctor. When he had finished his training he would be ready to go to China, where he would spend his life healing the sick, and telling the people about Jesus.

*   *   *   *   *   *

Thomas Barnardo worked hard in London, studying to become a doctor. But he still found time to help others, just as he had done in Dublin. He soon found slums in the East End of London like the slums of

Dublin, where people were poor and hungry.

Most of all he wanted to help children. He found lots of boys in the streets of the slums, hungry and thin, with only rags for clothes. There were no proper schools for children in those days, so Thomas Barnardo made up his mind that this was where he would start. He had heard about the Ragged Schools for boys, started by Lord Shaftesbury, the famous friend of the poor. Now Thomas Barnardo decided that he would start a school of his own. He called it the Donkey Shed Ragged School, for that was where it was held.

One cold winter's night a new boy called Jim Jarvis came to the school. When the evening was over and the boys had drunk their hot cocoa, they said goodnight and ran off to their homes. Then, just as Thomas Barnardo was about to turn out the lamp, he saw Jim Jarvis curled up behind a box beside the remains of the fire.

"Let me sleep 'ere," Jim pleaded.

"But you must go home!" said Thomas Barnardo.

"I ain't got no 'ome," said Jim.

Thomas Barnardo felt so sorry for Jim that he took him back to his own lodgings and saw that he had a good supper. He watched him as he bolted down the

food like a hungry wolf, and decided that he must
find out more about him.

Jim was ten years old, but he was so small and thin
that he looked much younger. He had no boots, no
socks, no underclothes and no cap. All he had was a
ragged coat and torn trousers. He had no home, and
no friends.

"There's lots of boys like me," Jim said, between
mouthfuls. "We eats anything and sleeps anywhere."

"Come and show me," said Thomas Barnardo.

They went out together into the cold night. Jim
searched and searched, but did not find any boys.

"I'm beginning to think this is just a story!" said
Thomas Barnardo.

"No, Gov'nor, it's true—honest!" said Jim. "We'll find 'em."

Then they went down an alley and climbed a high wall. "Look, Gov'nor!" whispered Jim. And in the pale moonlight, Thomas Barnardo saw eleven ragged boys huddled together for warmth on the flat roof of a shed.

*   *   *   *   *   *

Now Thomas Barnardo went out every night searching for ragged, homeless boys—"urchins" as they were called. He found many urchins like Jim, and made friends with them. He knew that he must do something to help them.

One night he went to a missionary meeting, just like the one in Dublin when he had decided to go to China. As it was about to begin, a message came to say that the missionary was ill and would not be able to give his talk after all. The man in charge of the meeting was very upset, for already the hall was packed with people. Then he thought of Thomas Barnardo, and he asked him to speak about his work for the children of the poor instead. "Tell them about your urchins," he said.

Thomas Barnardo talked for over an hour. His audience listened in silence, horrified by his incredible story. The next day the papers were full of it. Then people began to write angry letters to the papers. "Barnardo's story is not true!" they wrote. "He's making it up!"

The famous Lord Shaftesbury read the story and the letters. He invited Thomas Barnardo to come to his house to meet the people who did not believe the doctor's story. They all argued for a long time, then Lord Shaftesbury said, "We can soon settle this. It's nearly midnight—let's go and see for ourselves."

They went in hansom cabs to the slums of the East End of London, and that night they found seventy-three boys. The children were huddled together for

warmth, sleeping wherever they could find a place where the police would not see them.

As they were going back home, Lord Shaftesbury spoke to Thomas Barnardo. "You have found your 'China' here in London," he said. "Why sail away to the East to work for God when there is so much for you to do here? God bless you in your work for the urchins. You can rely on me to help you all I can."

* * * * * *

Thomas Barnardo qualified as a doctor, and in 1867 he set up his first Home for homeless boys. His Christian friends helped him with gifts of money to buy food and clothes and beds for his "family". It was only a small Home, and there was only room for a few boys.

One day a boy named Ginger came and pleaded to be taken in. He was thin and ragged and hungry— and he looked ill. But there was just no room for him, and Doctor Barnardo had to turn him away. A few days later there came terrible news—Ginger had died.

Doctor Barnardo was heartbroken. He made a solemn promise: "We will never again turn any child away," he said. "The door of the Home will be an

Ever Open Door." More and more orphan children came to his Home, and the door was never closed to any of them.

Doctor Barnardo had no money of his own, but he trusted in God that, somehow, the money he needed for his children would be found. And as more and more people heard of his Home at Stepney Causeway, in the East End of London, they sent money so that his work there could grow. Even babies were brought there, or left on the doorstep, and they too were taken in.

Then came a wonderful gift—a house at Hawkhurst in Kent was given to Doctor Barnardo for his work. He called it Babies' Castle, and it became a fine new Home for orphan babies.

*   *   *   *   *   *

As Doctor Barnardo's children grew up, they needed to be trained so that they could earn their living. Another house was given to Doctor Barnardo, and it became a Home for training boys who wanted to join the Royal Navy. Another Home for training girls was set up at Ilford in Essex, where they lived as families in separate cottages. Many of his children went to settle in Canada and Australia.

When Doctor Barnardo died in 1905, sixty thousand children had been brought up in his Homes. His work went on growing, and nowadays, just as when he was alive, children in need are cared for in the Homes which proudly bear his name.

He never became a missionary. He never went to China. But he *did* tell many people about Jesus, and he showed them God's love by giving his whole life to caring for them. He found his "China" in the backstreets of Britain by caring for the thousands of poor children who came into his Homes. The name of Doctor Thomas Barnardo lives on as the founder of the largest family in the world.

Rama and the King of Demons

Most people who follow the Hindu religion live in India, but wherever Hindu people live, they keep *Diwali,* which means "the festival of lights". This is the story that is told at the festival. It tells how, many years ago, good overcame evil, and light overcame darkness.

★　　★　　★　　★　　★　　★

Long ago, in the land of India, there lived a prince named Rama whose father ruled over the kingdom. Rama was the eldest son, so he would become king after his father.

One day Rama went to visit another kingdom where he met a beautiful princess named Sita. Rama fell in love with her at once.

Now Sita's father had made a promise—the first prince to break the huge wooden bow which stood outside his palace would have Princess Sita for his wife.

Rama was strong as well as clever, and he could see exactly what he had to do. The Princess Sita

watched Rama break the bow and, as she watched
him, she fell in love with him too. So Prince Rama
and Princess Sita were married, and it seemed that
they would live happily ever after.

*   *   *   *   *   *

But their happiness was soon to end, for Rama had a
cruel stepmother who had a son of her own. Rama's
stepmother wanted her own son to become king
instead of Rama, and she tricked the king into making
two promises. The first promise was that her own
son must be the next king. The second promise was
that Rama should be sent away from the kingdom to
live alone in the forests for fourteen years.

Now Rama had a brother called Lakshman. "You must fight for your kingdom!" he cried to Rama.

"No!" said Rama. "A royal promise must be kept, and I must obey my father."

"Then I will go to the forests with you," said Lakshman.

"And I too will go to the forests with you," said Sita.

"I cannot take you, dear Sita," said Rama sadly. "The forests are full of tribes of wild men and fierce animals. A princess cannot live among such dangers."

"I will follow you, my lord," said Sita, "even to the ends of the earth."

So Rama and Sita went to live in the forests, and Lakshman went with them. They wore rough clothes, and ate whatever food they could find—berries and fruits from trees, and plants and roots from the earth. They drank water from streams and rivers, and at night they slept under the trees.

One day Sita saw a golden deer among the trees. "I would love to have that deer," she said to Rama.

"Then I will capture it for you," said Rama. He ordered Lakshman to guard Sita and not to leave her for any reason at all. Then he hurried off to catch the golden deer.

Some time later, Sita and Lakshman heard a cry. It sounded like the voice of Rama crying, "Help! Lakshman, come and help me! I'm wounded!"

Lakshman did not want to leave Sita alone, but she ordered him to go and help Rama. No sooner had he gone than an old beggar came towards the shelter where Sita was waiting all alone.

"Anyone there?" he called. "An old beggar needs water to drink."

Kind Sita hurried out with her jug of water, and at once the beggar seized her. It was Ravana, the king of demons! It was he who had sent his servant, disguised as a deer, to lure Rama away. It was he who had imitated the voice of Rama. Now he was pretending to be a wandering beggar, so that he could capture Princess Sita. In vain the princess struggled to get free. The evil Ravana threw her over his shoulder and set off back to his kingdom, the island of Lanka.

When Rama found out what had happened he was heart-broken. He knew that he would need an army to storm the island of Lanka and to fight the evil Ravana. He asked Hanuman, the Monkey God, to help him. Hanuman sent him a great host of monkeys and Rama trained them to shoot with bows and arrows, and to march like soldiers. Now he had an army to fight the Demon King.

Rama had friends wherever he went, for he was friendly to all. Both animals and men were his friends. They all hated the evil Ravana, king of demons, and they gladly helped the good Prince Rama.

At last Rama reached the sea. Now he needed a bridge to cross to the island kingdom of Lanka, where the evil Ravana lived—and again the monkeys helped him. They threw rocks and stones into the sea to make a bridge to the island. Even the squirrels helped!

As soon as the bridge was finished, Rama and his army of monkeys crossed to the island where Sita was kept prisoner by the king of demons. Rama spoke to the people of the island. "My fight is only with Ravana your king," he cried. "If Ravana will give me back my wife Sita, I will go home tomorrow."

But the evil king would not give Sita back to Rama, so he had to fight for her. There was battle after battle, but at last the royal city was surrounded by Rama's great army, and Ravana and his soldiers were trapped. Rama and his men fought the soldiers of Ravana until they were all dead.

Then Ravana himself came out of the city gate. He hurled himself at Rama and fought like a madman. But Rama's arrow found his heart, and Ravana fell dead. And at the death of the Demon King, the heavens were filled with music and sweet-scented flowers poured down like rain from the sky.

Now, at last, Rama and Sita could return home.
Fourteen years had passed since they went out to live
in the forests, and many things had happened in that
time. The old king, Rama's father, had died, and
Rama's stepbrother had been made king by his
stepmother. But now Rama was returning—and *he*
was the true king. Rama's stepbrother was so happy
to see him again that he gladly gave the kingdom back
to him.

What rejoicing there was on the day that King
Rama and Queen Sita drove in their golden chariot
and sat on their thrones before all the people! There
had never been such a happy day. There had never
been such shouting and cheering, such singing and
dancing. How glad the people were to welcome them

back! Good King Rama and his wife Queen Sita had overcome the evil ruler of demons.

Their goodness was like the bright light of morning, and Ravana's evil was like the darkness of night. The good king and queen had overcome the evil demon, and light had overcome darkness. Now all the people were happy. They shouted and cheered, they sang and danced. And all around them, lights were lit to show how King Rama and Queen Sita had won the great victory of light over darkness.

*　　*　　*　　*　　*　　*

The people of India never forgot that day and that victory. It was remembered every year and it became part of the great festival of Diwali. This is the most important festival of the year for Hindu people. The whole family shares in Diwali and the story of Rama and Sita. Boys are told, "You must be good like King Rama." Girls are told, "You must be good like Queen Sita." And mothers and fathers want to be like them too!

Lights are lit in the home for the Festival of Lights, and rows of lights shine out in the streets. Fireworks and crackers are let off, and a huge dummy of Ravana, king of demons, is burnt on a great bonfire.

Diwali begins the New Year too, so everything must be new for the festival. Homes are cleaned, and special decorations are put up to make them look new. Pots and pans are polished in the kitchen, and everyone has new clothes, especially children.

Diwali is a time for giving presents, for sending good wishes to friends, and for having parties together. The most important party of all is when families meet together in their temple, all in their fine new clothes.

At their temple they sing the praises of Lord Rama and Queen Sita, and once again they hear the story of how good overcame evil, and how light overcame darkness.

Holy Places: Temple

People who follow the Hindu religion believe in
Brahman, which is their name for God. Brahman is
the Spirit of God which is everywhere, in all things
and in all people. Hindus believe that Brahman
makes himself known through many Gods and
Goddesses, who are worshipped at their own
temples. At Madura, in the south of India, there is
the great temple of the God named Shiva and of his
Goddess. Temples like these have stone carvings of
Hindu Gods and saints, as well as animals and people.

But wherever Hindus live, they have their temple,
which sometimes is just a small room, and they have
a statue of whichever God they worship. Worshippers
bow low before the statue to make their offerings and
to say their prayers.

The Kiss that Betrayed a King

One of the greatest festivals of the year for Christians is Easter. It includes Good Friday, when they remember how Jesus was killed by his enemies. This is the story of the first Good Friday.

*   *   *   *   *   *

The members of the Jewish Council were very worried when they met together. It was a special meeting to decide what to do about Jesus. The members were the Chief Priests, teachers of the Jewish Law, and important religious leaders called Pharisees. Caiaphas the High Priest was in charge of the Council, which was allowed by the Romans to rule over the Jews.

"What are we going to do about Jesus?" asked one speaker. "He is a threat to all of us. He is popular among the people because of his teaching and because he heals the sick. If we let him go on like this, he will become their leader—and that will anger the Romans. They let our Council rule the people— but only as long as there is no trouble. If the Romans even suspect there may be an uprising against them, they will show us no mercy. They will destroy us—and that will be the end of our people!"

Other speakers agreed with him. They were all very worried about what the Romans might do. Caiaphas the High Priest listened to them for some time. Then he stood up and everyone fell silent.

"You do not understand the matter," he said to the Council. "It is quite simple. One man must die in order that the people may live. Jesus must die to save our people from being destroyed."

Yes, that was the answer. The Council agreed with the High Priest, and they began to make plans for getting rid of Jesus.

★　　★　　★　　★　　★　　★

Jesus had come to Jerusalem for the week of the Passover Festival. Each day he spoke to the people in the Festival. Each day he spoke to the people in the courts of the Temple, which was crowded with Jews from all over the world. Important men asked Jesus cunning questions, trying to trap him.

"Master," they said, very politely, "we know that you teach the way of God and never hide the truth. Tell us—is it right to pay taxes to the Romans? Should we pay them or not?"

It was a clever question. If Jesus said it was wrong to pay Roman taxes, they could arrest him at once and hand him over to the Romans as a traitor. If Jesus said that it was right to pay Roman taxes he would anger the people—and that would be the end of him as a popular leader.

But Jesus could see through their cunning. "Why do you try to trick me?" he said to them. "Bring me a Roman coin." When the coin was brought, Jesus held it out on the palm of his hand. The coin was stamped with the head of the Roman emperor, with his name stamped in letters around it.

"Whose face and whose name is this?" Jesus asked them.

"The emperor's," they answered.

"Then give to the emperor what belongs to the emperor, and give to God what belongs to God." The people were amazed at the clever answer that Jesus gave. And his questioners slunk away.

*   *   *   *   *   *

The Chief Priests dared not try to arrest Jesus whilst he was so popular with the people. That would be sure to cause a riot. Somehow they had to lay hands on him when he was alone. Their chance came through Judas Iscariot, one of the twelve disciples of Jesus. He went secretly to the chief priests and offered to betray Jesus to them for money. They were delighted.

"We will pay you thirty pieces of silver," they said. Judas agreed and from then on he looked for a time to betray Jesus.

*   *   *   *   *   *

On the evening of the following day Jesus was alone with his little group of disciples on the Mount of Olives, just outside Jerusalem. They were in the quiet garden called Gethsemane. There Jesus prayed,

deeply troubled as he thought of what lay ahead for
him.

Suddenly, there came the sound of voices, and
lights flickered among the trees. Judas knew that Jesus
would be in his favourite garden at this time. He led
the guards of the High Priest, armed with swords
and clubs, and carrying torches. Then he went up to
Jesus and gave him the kiss of friendship.

"Hail, Master!" he cried—and that was the signal
for the men to seize Jesus. They bound his hands
together, and led him back to the city.

And all the disciples of Jesus ran away.

The guards led Jesus to the house of the High Priest, who began to ask Jesus questions about his followers and about his teaching.

"I have always spoken openly," Jesus answered. "I taught people in the synagogues and in the courts of the Temple. Why ask me these questions? Why not ask those who heard me? They will know best what I said."

Immediately an officer of the guard struck Jesus. "Is that the way to speak to the High Priest?" he cried.

"If I have said something wrong, say what it is," Jesus answered him. "But if I spoke the truth, why strike me?"

Jesus made no reply to the questions. He would not say a word to defend himself, and at last the guards led him away with his hands still tied.

*   *   *   *   *   *

The High Priest Caiaphas had gathered members of the Council together to try Jesus. They had to get evidence against him and find him guilty before they could sentence him to death. There were plenty of witnesses to speak against Jesus. Some of them had been paid to tell lies—but since their lies did not agree, the Council could not find him guilty.

There was no time to lose for it was already Friday. The Jewish day began and ended at sunset. In a few hours it would be Saturday, the holy sabbath, when no work of any kind could be done. They had to find Jesus guilty and sentence him to death by sunset at the latest. But they had found no proof that Jesus had broken any law. Nor would he defend himself. He remained silent.

The High Priest decided he would have to question Jesus himself. He got up and came and stood before the rest of them. "Have you nothing to say?" he cried. "What answer do you have to all these charges against you?"

Still Jesús stood silent. Then Caiaphas asked him directly, "Are you the Saviour, the Son of God?"

At last Jesus answered him, in words from the sacred writings of the Jews: "I am. And you will see the Son of Man sitting at the right hand of God, and coming with the clouds of heaven."

"Blasphemy!" cried the High Priest. "The prisoner has mocked God!" With both hands, Caiaphas tore open the top of his tunic to show his horror at what Jesus had said. "What need is there for further witness?" he cried to the members of the Council. "You heard his blasphemy—what is your verdict?"

"Guilty!" they cried. "Jesus must die!"

Then some of them began to spit on Jesus. Others blindfolded him, struck his face with the palms of their hands and shouted, "Now, you prophet, tell us who slapped you!" Even the guards joined in.

By now it was daybreak, and the whole Council was there. They gave their solemn verdict. Jesus was guilty of blasphemy—a crime against God. The penalty by Jewish law was death. They could get rid of Jesus, once and for all!

*　　*　　*　　*　　*　　*

The Romans did not permit the Jewish Council to

put anyone to death. Only Pontius Pilate, the Roman Governor, could order sentence of death. So the Chief Priests would have to persuade Pilate that Jesus was guilty. They knew that Romans believed in many Gods, and Pilate did not care about the God of the Jews. Blasphemy against their God was not important to him. But if the Chief Priests could show that Jesus was guilty of treason against Rome, that would be a very different matter. Pilate would take that very seriously.

The Chief Priests had sent a message to Pilate about the important prisoner they wanted him to sentence. He was waiting at the Roman headquarters when they arrived with Jesus and his guards.

They told Pilate of their charges against Jesus. "This is the man. He leads our people astray. He tells them that it is wrong to pay Roman taxes. He even claims to be our king!"

Pilate turned to Jesus. "Are you the king of the Jews?" he asked.

"Yes, I am," Jesus answered. The Roman governor could see that the prisoner was no wild rebel against Rome. If he *was* a king, he certainly was not an earthly king.

Pilate did not believe the charges brought against

Jesus. He turned back to the Chief Priests. "I find this man not guilty of any crime against Rome," he said firmly.

But the Chief Priests shouted back, " He is a trouble-maker! He stirred up the people in Galilee, and now he's causing trouble here in Jerusalem."

When Pilate heard that Jesus came from Galilee, he saw an easy way out for himself. King Herod ruled over Galilee, so anyone from there could be tried by him. Herod was in Jerusalem for the festival too. So Pilate sent Jesus to him for trial.

King Herod was very pleased. He had heard a lot about Jesus and had wanted to meet him for a long time. He began by asking Jesus questions. But Jesus did not answer him. Members of the Council stood by, shouting their charges against Jesus. But he would not defend himself.

Herod was very disappointed. He had hoped that Jesus would perform some great wonder—but he would not even speak! So Herod and his soldiers mocked Jesus. They dressed him up like a king with a fine cloak, and made fun of him. Then Herod sent him back to Pilate, saying that he could get nothing from the prisoner. The Roman Governor was going to have to decide the case himself.

The Chief Priests brought Jesus back to Pilate, who came out and sat on his judgement-seat.

"You have accused this man of being a trouble-maker," he said to the chief priests. "I have examined him and find him not guilty of any crime. Herod has found nothing against him either. I will therefore set him free."

But the Chief Priests and their crowd yelled, "Away with him! Away with him!"

Pontius Pilate was convinced that Jesus had done nothing to deserve death. He wanted to let him go, so he said again, "This man has committed no crime against Rome. He must be set free."

But the crowd shouted back, "Crucify him! Crucify him!"

Pilate tried once more. He had another prisoner called Barabbas, who was a rebel. He had led a riot, and even committed murder. He deserved to die twice over—but he was very popular.

"As you know," Pilate said to the people, "it is a custom at the Passover Festival that I give one prisoner his freedom. Now who do you want me to set free—Barabbas, or Jesus the King?"

"Barabbas!" they shouted. "We want Barabbas!"

Pilate could see that Jesus was innocent. But he could also see trouble ahead for himself if he did not give the chief priests what they were demanding. Jerusalem was packed with excited Jews who had come from all over the world to celebrate the Passover Festival. If a riot broke out in the crowded city during the festival, he knew that he would never be able to control it. So, in the end, Pilate gave in to the demands of the chief priests and their crowd.

Pilate signed two orders—one for Barabbas to be freed, the other for Jesus to be crucified. He ordered a notice to be put over the cross of Jesus with these words on it: THIS IS JESUS
THE KING OF THE JEWS

Christians, the followers of Jesus, have never forgotten that Friday when Jesus died on the Cross. But Christians also believe that Jesus came alive again on the third day, and now lives for evermore. Every year, at the Festival of Easter, Christians remember the time when Jesus died on the Cross on Good Friday, and how he rose again on Easter Sunday. So the festival which begins with such sad memories ends with the joyful and triumphant belief that Jesus is alive—and that he lives for evermore in the hearts and lives of those who believe in him.

Holy Places: Gate to Heaven

The ancient religion of Japan is called Shinto, which means Way of the Gods.

The greatest Goddess of all is the Sun-Goddess, and her temple is the holiest place in all Japan. The Sun-Goddess was believed to be the ancestor of the emperors of Japan.

There are other holy places besides temples, like Mount Fuji, which is the home of another Goddess. On paths leading to holy places, and in front of each temple, there is a "Gate to Heaven", or "torii". Usually these gateways were made of plain wood, but the gateways in front of the temples of Inari, the God of Food, were always painted red. Modern gateways are sometimes made of bronze.

The people of Japan believe that these gates lead to heaven, and they bow to honour the Gods as they pass through them.